My guided
GARDEN PLANNER
log book & journal

NAME

....

Copyright

Copyright © 2023 Sophie McKay

Published in the United States of America, 2023
Legal Notice: This book is copyright protected. This book is only for personal use. All rights reserved. No portion of this book may be reproduced, stored in a retrieval system, or transmitted in any form or by any means – electronic, mechanical, photocopy, recording, or any other – except for brief quotations in a book review, without the prior written permission of the author or publisher.

For more information, contact www.sophiemckay.com
First edition, 2023
ISBN 978-1-916662-06-3 (paperback)

Website: www.SophieMcKay.com
Email: Sophie@sophiemckay.com
Author page: https://www.facebook.com/Sophie.McKay.Author
Facebook: www.facebook.com/groups/garden.to.table.tribe

How to Use This Journal

Welcome to your new guided gardening journal and logbook! I created this book to help you keep track of your gardening journey and give you helpful advice along the way. You may wonder how to begin, but don't worry; it's simple!

First, familiarize yourself with the book's various parts, such as the goal list, seed inventory, and garden layout planner. Then, begin filling in the details pertinent to your garden. You don't have to complete everything at once. Take your time and appreciate the process of brainstorming, observing and tracking your progress. Remember, this book is here to assist you and keep you organized, so relax, keep it simple, and have fun.

One of the many advantages of keeping notes in your journal is that you can return to them next year and replicate your successes. Furthermore, if you faced any problems last year, you can learn from them and make changes for future gardening seasons.

Use this book to record exciting things that happen in your garden and to remind you of things you want to attempt in the future. I've also included some drawings in the book that you can color in to personalize your diary. Use this journal to enjoy your creativity while relaxing in the garden.

Good luck and happy gardening!

Sophie

Table of contents

Plans for The Year	6
What do I want from my dream garden?	7
Goals Planner and Action Plan	9
Tools Inventory and Shopping List	12
Seed, Root, and Bulb Inventory	13
My Wish List	15
My Shopping List	16
My Favorite Nurseries and Suppliers	17
Family Food Needs Tracker	20
Garden Expense Tracker	24
The no-spend challenge	26
Know Your Place! Garden Notes and Observations	27
Garden Layout and Sun Map	28
Garden Notes and Observations	31
Garden Bed Planner	33
Sowing Calendar	37
Seed Starting Log	38
My Calendar	40
Planting, Blooming, and Harvesting Timeline	48
Early Spring : Seasonal Chore Planner, Tasks and Review	52
Late Spring : Seasonal Chore Planner, Tasks and Review	54
Early Summer : Seasonal Chore Planner, Tasks and Review	57
Late Summer : Seasonal Chore Planner, Tasks and Review	59
Fall: Seasonal Chore Planner, Tasks and Review	62
Winter: Seasonal Chore Planner, Tasks and Review	65
Square-Foot Gardening Basics	68
My Square Foot Garden	69
Companion Planting Quick Guide	74
Crop Rotation Plan	77
Grow Bag Cheat Sheet	80
Plant Profiles	82
Composting Basics	103
Rainfall Recording Sheet and Watering Tracker	105
Water Saving Ideas for the Future	108
Pest and Disease Tracker	109
Pollinator Fan Page	112
Link to download free, printable pages for your log book	119
Notes	120
Dot Grid Planner	129
Ready for some more inspiration?	137

My Quick Links
(my personal table of contents)

Plans for The Year

You can use this page to brainstorm and plan what you want to achieve in your garden this year. Write your thoughts into the speech bubbles on the next page. Bring together all your ideas and inspirations for your space, and summarize your final decisions below.

Remember, it's important to set simple and realistic goals, so you don't feel overwhelmed. Think about what you want from your garden. For example, do you want to grow your own food, create a relaxing outdoor space, or attract pollinators?

Once you've decided on your goals, it's time to come up with a plan to reach them. Maybe you need to do some research on plant varieties, invest in some new tools, or start a compost pile.

Don't forget to keep notes throughout the season so that you can repeat successful strategies and learn from any challenges.

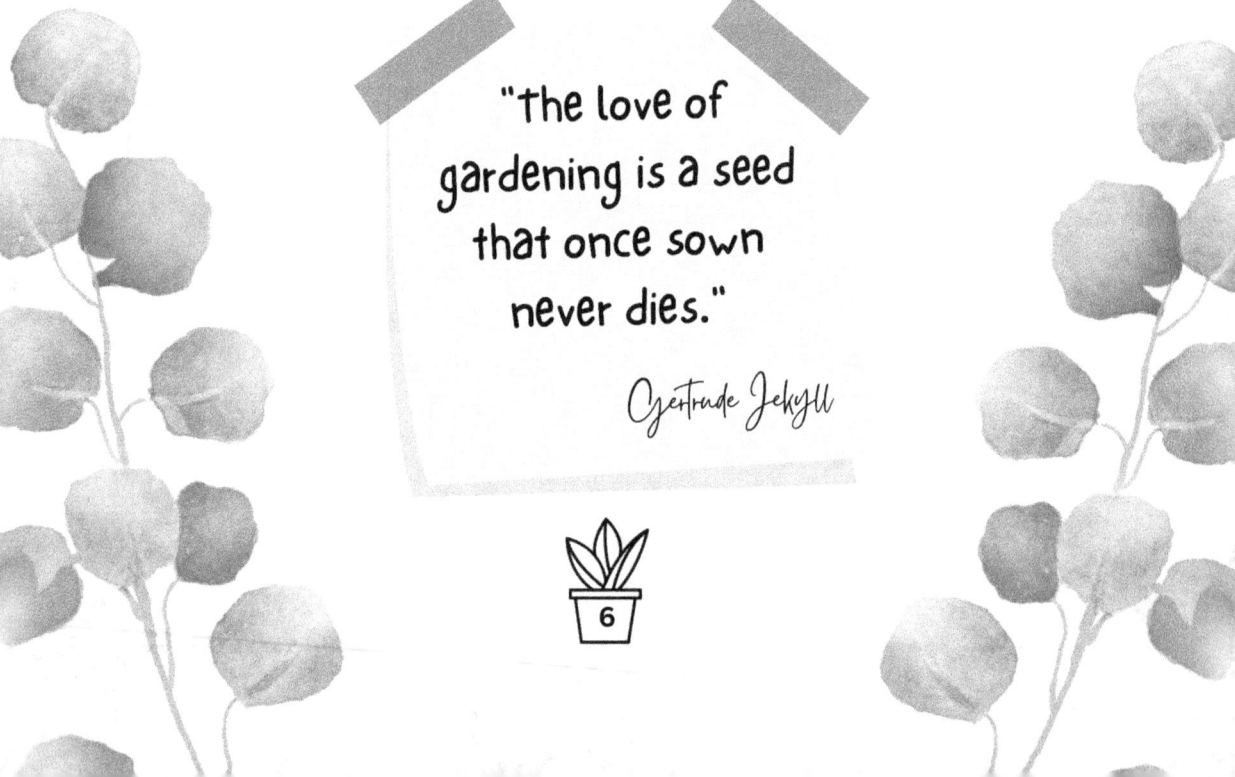

"the love of gardening is a seed that once sown never dies."

Gertrude Jekyll

Brainstorming Page
What do I want from my dream garden?

Brainstorming Page
What do I want from my dream garden?

Final decisions

Goals Planner and Action Plan

Use this page to break down your garden goals into actionable tasks. Having your goals broken down into more achievable sections will help you avoid stress and procrastination, but remember that you can always change things if needed.

MY MAIN GARDENING GOAL:
....
....
....

MILESTONE / STEP 1	MILESTONE / STEP 2	MILESTONE / STEP 3

ACTIONS	ACTIONS	ACTIONS
☐	☐	☐ ....
☐	☐	☐ ....
☐	☐	☐ ....
☐	☐	☐ ....
☐	☐	☐ ....
☐	☐	☐ ....
☐	☐	☐ ....
☐	☐	☐ ....

TARGET DATE ☐	TARGET DATE ☐	TARGET DATE ☐

Goals Planner and Action Plan

MY GARDENING GOAL:

....
....
....
....

MILESTONE / STEP 1	MILESTONE / STEP 2	MILESTONE / STEP 3

ACTIONS	ACTIONS	ACTIONS
☐	☐	☐
☐	☐	☐
☐	☐	☐
☐	☐	☐
☐	☐	☐
☐	☐	☐
☐	☐	☐
☐	☐	☐
TARGET DATE ☐	TARGET DATE ☐	TARGET DATE ☐

Goals Planner and Action Plan

MY GARDENING GOAL:

....
....
....
....

MILESTONE / STEP 1	MILESTONE / STEP 2	MILESTONE / STEP 3

ACTIONS	ACTIONS	ACTIONS
☐	☐	☐ ....
☐	☐	☐ ....
☐	☐	☐ ....
☐	☐	☐ ....
☐	☐	☐ ....
☐	☐	☐ ....
☐	☐	☐ ....
☐	☐	☐ ....

TARGET DATE ☐	TARGET DATE ☐	TARGET DATE ☐

Tools Inventory and Shopping List

At the start of the season, check your garden tools! Mark the tools you already have and don't need to be fixed or changed. Below you can create a list of what you still need to purchase.

Seed, Root, and Bulb Inventory

PLANT	VARIETY	QTY	PURCHASED	ORIGIN	BUY AGAIN?

Seed, Root, and Bulb Inventory

PLANT	VARIETY	QTY	PURCHASED	ORIGIN	BUY AGAIN?

My Wish List

SEEDS AND PLANTS
- [ ]
- [ ]
- [ ]
- [ ]
- [ ]
- [ ]
- [ ]
- [ ]
- [ ]

GARDEN TOOLS
- [ ]
- [ ]
- [ ]
- [ ]
- [ ]
- [ ]
- [ ]
- [ ]
- [ ]

SUPPLIES
- [ ]
- [ ]
- [ ]
- [ ]
- [ ]
- [ ]
- [ ]
- [ ]
- [ ]

OTHERS
- [ ]
- [ ]
- [ ]
- [ ]
- [ ]
- [ ]
- [ ]
- [ ]

My Shopping List

SEEDS AND PLANTS	GARDEN TOOLS
☐	☐
☐	☐
☐	☐
☐	☐
☐	☐
☐	☐
☐	☐
☐	☐
☐	☐

SUPPLIES	OTHERS
☐	☐
☐	☐
☐	☐
☐	☐
☐	☐
☐	☐
☐	☐
☐	☐
☐	☐

My Favorite Nurseries and Suppliers

Name: .... Phone:................................ Email: .... Address: .... Notes:	Name: .... Phone:................................ Email: .... Address: .... Notes: ....
Name: .... Phone:................................ Email: .... Address: .... Notes:	Name: .... Phone:................................ Email: .... Address: .... Notes: ....
Name: .... Phone:................................ Email: .... Address: .... Notes:	Name: .... Phone:................................ Email: .... Address: .... Notes: ....
Name: .... Phone:................................ Email: .... Address: .... Notes:	Name: .... Phone:................................ Email: .... Address: .... Notes: ....

My Favorite Nurseries and Suppliers

Name: ....
Phone: ....
Email: ....
Address: ....
Notes: ....

Name: ....
Phone: ....
Email: ....
Address: ....
Notes: ....

Name: ....
Phone: ....
Email: ....
Address: ....
Notes: ....

Name: ....
Phone: ....
Email: ....
Address: ....
Notes: ....

Name: ....
Phone: ....
Email: ....
Address: ....
Notes: ....

Name: ....
Phone: ....
Email: ....
Address: ....
Notes: ....

Name: ....
Phone: ....
Email: ....
Address: ....
Notes: ....

Name: ....
Phone: ....
Email: ....
Address: ....
Notes: ....

My Favorite Nurseries and Suppliers

Name: .... Phone: .... Email: .... Address: .... Notes:	Name: .... Phone: .... Email: .... Address: .... Notes: ....
Name: .... Phone: .... Email: .... Address: .... Notes:	Name: .... Phone: .... Email: .... Address: .... Notes: ....
Name: .... Phone: .... Email: .... Address: .... Notes:	Name: .... Phone: .... Email: .... Address: .... Notes: ....
Name: .... Phone: .... Email: .... Address: .... Notes:	Name: .... Phone: .... Email: .... Address: .... Notes: ....

Family Food Needs Tracker

A food requirements tracker can help you plan and cultivate your own veggies at home. You may decide how much of each vegetable you need to grow by measuring the number/quantity of vegetables your family consumes each week.

This helps you to design your garden, ensuring that you grow the crops your family appreciates the most. For example, if your household needs two pounds of tomatoes per week, you may figure that 12 tomato plants are required to supply that need during the growing season. You could also choose to grow more than you need and preserve/store some for later!

The precise quantity and number of plants required will vary based on your family's needs and tastes, the variety of your chosen plant, and the growth circumstances in your location. Here's an example of a basic table you could use to keep track of your family's dietary requirements. You can start with this table and change the numbers as needed to build a personalized plan for your garden.

Vegetables Fruits	Amount needed per week	Monthly amount	Avg yield of 1 plant of the chosen variety	Number of plants needed per season
Lettuce (head)	2 pcs	8 pcs	1 head per planting	24 plants
Tomato	3 pounds	12 pounds	8-20 pounds / plant variety	6-8 plants
Zucchini	3 pounds	12 pounds	3-10 pounds / plant variety	4-8 plants

Family Food Needs Tracker

Vegetables Fruits	Amount needed per week	Monthly amount	Avg yield of 1 plant of the chosen variety	Number of plants needed per season

Family Food Needs Tracker

Vegetables Fruits	Amount needed per week	Monthly amount	Avg yield of 1 plant of the chosen variety	Number of plants needed per season

Family Food Needs Tracker

Vegetables Fruits	Amount needed per week	Monthly amount	Avg yield of 1 plant of the chosen variety	Number of plants needed per season

Garden Expense Tracker

DATE	ITEM / DESCRIPTION	QTY	PLANNED COST	ACTUAL COST
			TOTAL	

NOTES

Garden Expense Tracker

DATE	ITEM / DESCRIPTION	QTY	PLANNED COST	ACTUAL COST

	TOTAL	

NOTES

The no-spend challenge

A no-spend challenge for gardeners not only encourages using what you already have but also promotes community building and sharing resources. Gardeners can exchange plants and seeds, or even borrow tools with their neighbors, creating a community and reducing waste by avoiding unnecessary purchases.

START DATE.................................... END DATE..

RULES:
....
....
....
....
....
....
....
....

MY DO NOT BUY LIST

☐ ....
☐ ....
☐ ....
☐ ....
☐ ....
☐ ....
☐ ....

EXCEPTIONALS FROM THE RULES

Know Your Place!
Garden Notes and Observations

Observing your garden or even your patio or balcony is critical to planning and building a good growing place. You can discover the optimum sites for plants and other garden equipment by spending time in your outside space and monitoring the patterns of sunshine, shadow, and wind.

For example, if you see that one region of your garden receives full light for most of the day, you can plan to plant sun-loving veggies or herbs there. If, on the other hand, you observe that a certain corner of your yard/balcony is always shaded, you can pick shade-tolerant plants that will grow in that setting.

Using these designs will help you maximize your available area and create a beautiful, healthy garden, regardless of how big or tiny it is.

Zone	Time			
	9 AM	11 AM	2 PM	6 PM
West wall	Shade	Partial sun	Very hot - full sun	Full sun
Vegetable garden	Partial sun	Sun	Sun	Sun
Apple tree area	Shade	Shade	Partial sun	Shade
Windowshill	Sun	Sun	Partial sun	Shade
Fireplace	Shade	Shade	Sunny - often windy	Sunny - often windy

Garden Layout and Sun Map

You can draw your backyard, garden, patio or even your balcony here. Don't worry too much about how precise your drawing is. Remember, the most important thing is to observe and understand your place.

Garden Layout and Sun Map

You can draw your backyard, garden, patio or even your balcony here. Don't worry too much about how precise your drawing is. Remember, the most important thing is to observe and understand your site.

Garden Layout and Sun Map

You can draw your backyard, garden, patio or even your balcony here. Don't worry too much about how precise your drawing is. Remember, the most important thing is to observe and understand your site.

Garden Notes and Observations

You can make notes about the different areas on your property. This will help you choose the best plants for each zone.

Zone	Time			

Garden Notes and Observations

You can make notes about the different areas on your property. This will help you choose the best plants for each zone.

Zone	Time			

Garden Bed Planner

Once you've identified your property's different zones and sun exposure areas, you can start designing your garden bed layouts.
One helpful approach is sketching your garden outline and experimenting with different plant arrangements for each area.

By considering factors like plant size, growth habits, and water needs, you can create a beautiful and functional garden that suits your property's unique characteristics.

Year: *2023*   Season: *Summer*

Garden Bed Planner

Year: Season:

Garden Bed Planner

Year: Season:

Garden Bed Planner

Year: Season:

Sowing calendar

January
Outside: Nothing
Indoors: cauliflower seeds, turnip greens, radishes, lettuce seeds, spinach seeds

February
Early peas
Indoors: cucumber plants, red and white cabbage, kohlrabi seeds, radishes seeds, celery

March
Rocket (one early & one late sowing)
Bronze arrowhead lettuce
Parsel, Mangetout
Tomatoes, Peppers, Thyme on the windowsill inside

April
Rocket (two sowings)
Bronze arrowhead lettuce
Parsley
Carrots (two sowings)
Basil (on windowsill inside)

May
Mizuna
Carrots (two sowings)
Plant out: tomatoes, peppers, thyme
Courgettes on the windowsill inside
Plant out basil

June
Carrots (two sowings), Mizuna
Plant out courgettes, Cauliflower, pointed cabbage, Chinese cabbage, minaret cauliflower

July
Mizuna and 2nd sow of: eets, Radishes, carrots, chives and carrot parsley. Green beans

August
Mizuna, rocket seeds, spinach seeds, winter purslane seeds, ramenas seeds, Rocket

September
Mizuna (for overwintering under cover)
Rocket / Lettuce / Spinach (for overwintering under cover or outside)

October
Garlic

Prepare the garden for the winter!

Seed Starting Log

Seeds I'll be starting indoors.

Crop/Seed	Date Planted	Date Germinated	Date Transplanted	Additional Notes

Seed Starting Log

Seeds I'll be starting indoors.

Crop/Seed	Date Planted	Date Germinated	Date Transplanted	Additional Notes

MY CALENDAR

JANUARY

FEBRUARY

MARCH

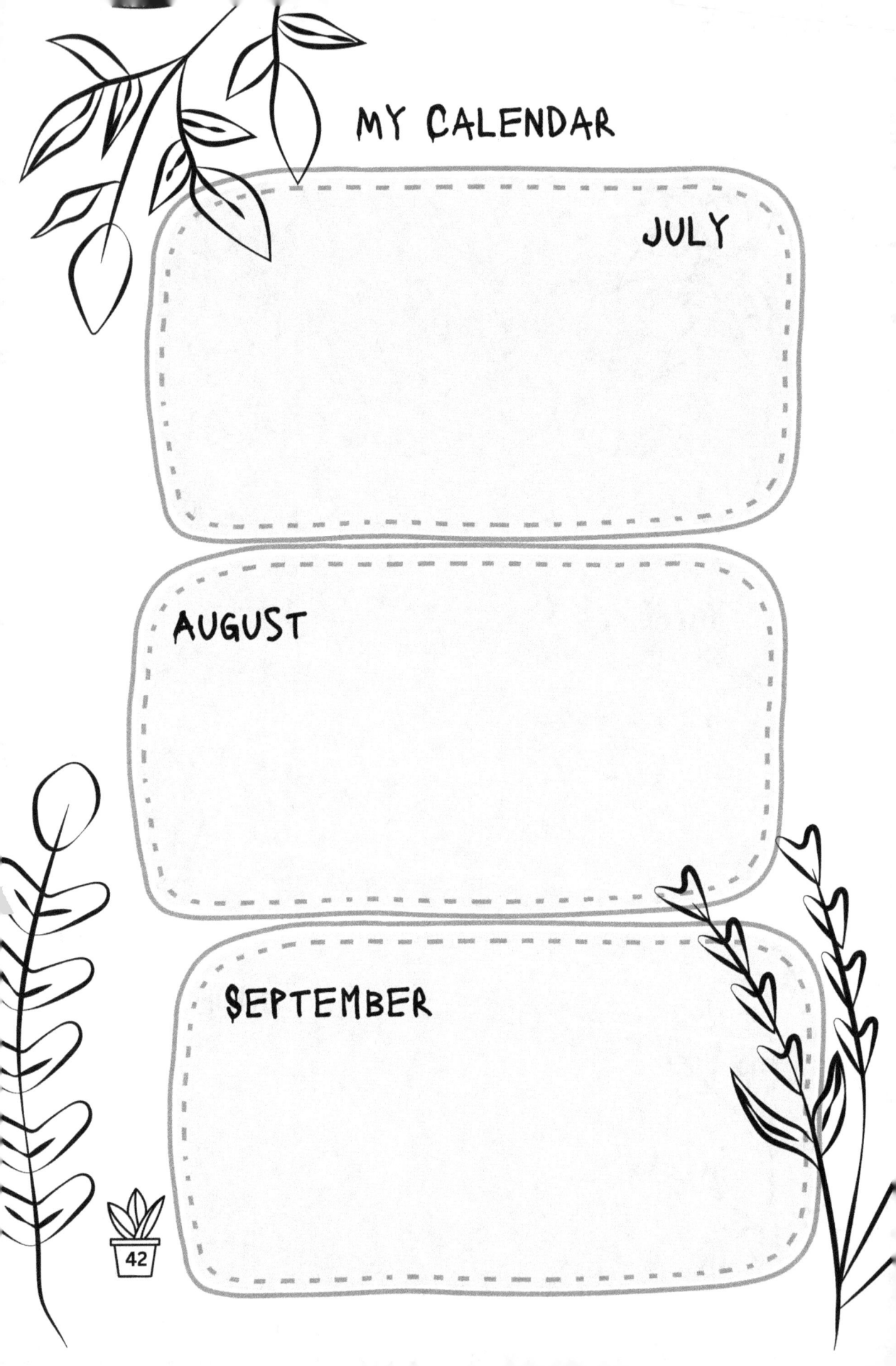

MY CALENDAR

JULY

AUGUST

SEPTEMBER

MY CALENDAR

OCTOBER

NOVEMBER

DECEMBER

MY CALENDAR

MY CALENDAR

MY CALENDAR

Planting, Blooming, and Harvesting Timeline

A garden timeline is a great way to stay organized and motivated throughout the gardening season. You can start by marking your zone's first and last frost dates. Then, as the season goes on, note the key stages of your plant's life cycle, as well as the major tasks you need to do.

This could include planting, germination, transplanting, pruning, fertilizing, and harvesting. For each stage, note down the dates, and which tasks that needed to be done and when.

For example, if you're growing tomatoes, you might include planting the seeds in early spring, transplanting the seedlings outdoors in late spring, pruning the plants in early summer, and harvesting the ripe fruit in late summer.

You can draw, color, or simply make notes. Give it a try and see how it can transform your gardening experience!

Plant name	JAN	FEB	MAR	APR	MAY	JUN	JUL	AUG	SEP	OCT	NOV	DEC
Tomato		❄	🌱		✻	🧺	🧺	🧺	🧺	❄		
Celeriac		❄		🌱					🧺	❄		
Chili		❄		🌱	✻	🧺	🧺		❄			
Lettuce		❄	🌱	🧺		🧺	🧺		🌱	❄		

❄ First and last frost dates of your zone: don't plant tender plants outside after the first or before the last frost dates!

🌱 Planting time: start seeds indoors/ plant outside

✻ Blooming: register the plant's blooming time

🧺 Harvesting period: mark the harvest periods!

Seasonal Chore Planner

Early Spring	Outdoors	Shade
Sow	corn salad, fennel, kale, kohlrabi, leeks, lettuce, onions, parsley, peas, arugula, beets, carrots, chives, chop suey greens, cilantro, radishes, scallions, spinach, Swiss chard, tarragon	carrots, celery root, corn, cucumbers, dwarf French beans, eggplants, lettuce, microgreens, alpine strawberries, arugula, basil, beets, peppers, tomatoes
Plant	chives, fruit trees and bushes, garlic, mint, onion and shallot sets, potatoes, rhubarb, tarragon	citrus trees
Harvest	chives, kale, leeks, microgreens, parsley, rhubarb, rosemary, sage, Swiss chard, thyme, windowsill herbs	

My plans

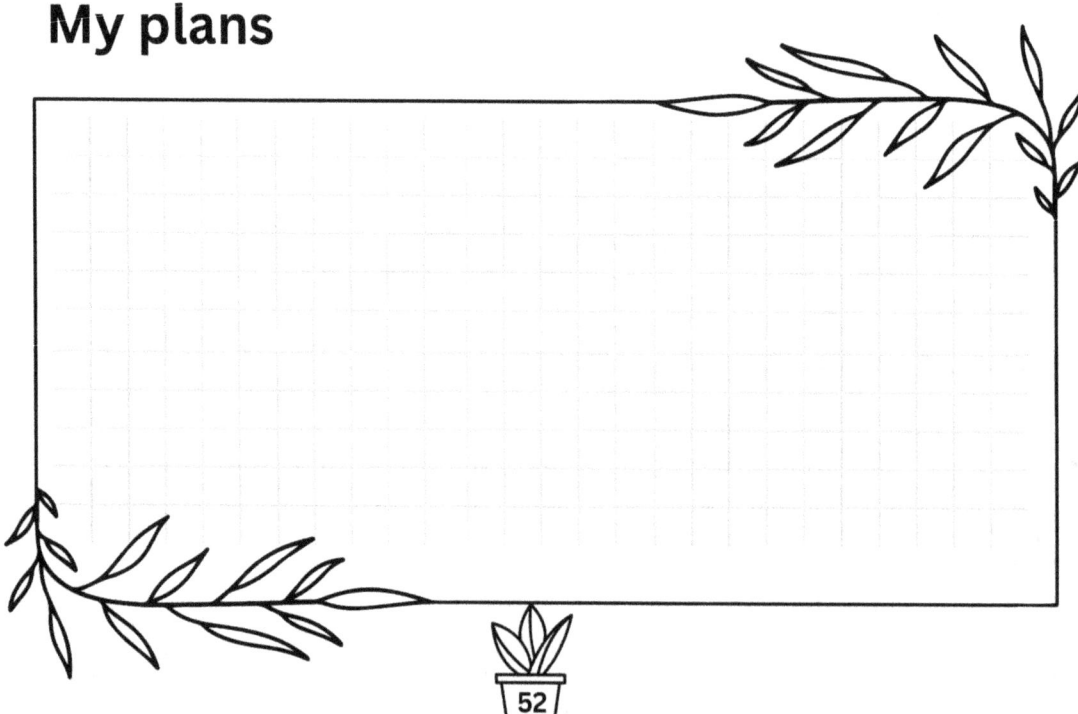

My Early Spring Tasks

Season:

Garden Beds/Row
- [ ]
- [ ]
- [ ]
- [ ]
- [ ]
- [ ]
- [ ]
- [ ]
- [ ]

Maintenance
- [ ]
- [ ]
- [ ]
- [ ]
- [ ]
- [ ]
- [ ]
- [ ]
- [ ]

Fertilizers
- [ ]
- [ ]
- [ ]
- [ ]
- [ ]
- [ ]
- [ ]
- [ ]
- [ ]
- [ ]

Planting/Harvesting
- [ ]
- [ ]
- [ ]
- [ ]
- [ ]
- [ ]
- [ ]
- [ ]
- [ ]

Seasonal Chore Planner

Late Spring

	Outdoors	Shade
Sow	American cress, arugula, beets, carrots, chicory, cilantro, corn, endive, Florence fennel, green beans, kale, kohlrabi, lettuce, mizuna, spinach, oregano, oriental mustard greens, parsley, peas, radicchio, radishes, runner beans, scallions, Swiss chard, thyme	basil, corn, cucumbers, eggplants, green beans, microgreens, runner beans, squashes, summer purslane, zucchini
Plant	Alpine strawberries, celery root, fennel, green beans, leeks, lettuce, mint, oregano, parsley, potatoes, rosemary, runner beans, thyme	citrus fruit, cucumbers, eggplants, peppers, tomatoes
Harvest	arugula, basil, beets, carrots, chives, chop suey greens, cilantro, fennel, gooseberries, kohlrabi, microgreens, mint, oregano, parsley, peas, radishes, rhubarb, rosemary, sage, scallions, spinach, strawberries, tarragon, thyme	

My plans

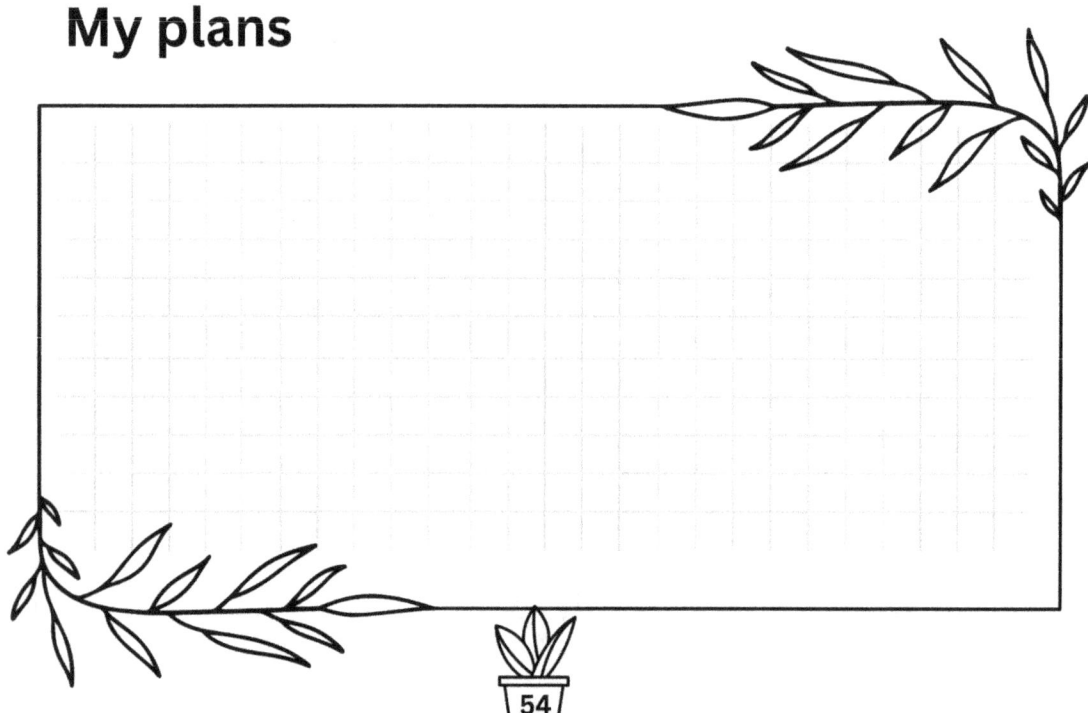

My Late Spring Tasks

Season:

Garden Beds/Row

- [ ]
- [ ]
- [ ]
- [ ]
- [ ]
- [ ]
- [ ]
- [ ]
- [ ]

Maintenance

- [ ]
- [ ]
- [ ]
- [ ]
- [ ]
- [ ]
- [ ]
- [ ]
- [ ]
- [ ]

Fertilizers

- [ ]
- [ ]
- [ ]
- [ ]
- [ ]
- [ ]
- [ ]
- [ ]
- [ ]

Planting/Harvesting

- [ ]
- [ ]
- [ ]
- [ ]
- [ ]
- [ ]
- [ ]
- [ ]
- [ ]
- [ ]

Seasonal Review: Spring

Plants harvested this season

Plants to try next season

What worked this season

What to do differently next season

Additional notes from this growing season

Seasonal Chore Planner

Early Summer

	Outdoors	Shade
Sow	American cress, arugula, beets, bokchoy, carrots, chicory, chop suey greens, cilantro, corn, corn salad, cucumbers, endive, green beans, kale, kohlrabi, lettuce, mizuna, oregano, oriental mustard greens, peas, radicchio, radishes, runner beans, scallions, spinach, squashes, tarragon, Witloof chicory, zucchini	basil, microgreens
Plant	celery root, corn, cucumbers, Florence fennel, kale, leeks, peppers, rosemary, squashes, tomatoes, zucchini	citrus fruit, cucumbers, eggplants, peppers, tomatoes
Harvest	American cress, arugula, basil, beets, carrots, cherries, chives, chop suey greens, corn salad, cucumbers, currants, fennel, gooseberries, herbs, kohlrabi, lettuce, microgreens, spinach, oregano, oriental mustard greens, peas, early potatoes, radicchio, radishes, rosemary, scallions, strawberries, Swiss chard, zucchini	

My plans

My Early Summer Tasks

Season:

Garden Beds/Row
- [ ]
- [ ]
- [ ]
- [ ]
- [ ]
- [ ]
- [ ]
- [ ]
- [ ]

Maintenance
- [ ]
- [ ]
- [ ]
- [ ]
- [ ]
- [ ]
- [ ]
- [ ]
- [ ]

Fertilizers
- [ ]
- [ ]
- [ ]
- [ ]
- [ ]
- [ ]
- [ ]
- [ ]
- [ ]

Planting/Harvesting
- [ ]
- [ ]
- [ ]
- [ ]
- [ ]
- [ ]
- [ ]
- [ ]
- [ ]

Seasonal Chore Planner

Late Summer

Outdoors

Sow: American cress, arugula, beets, bokchoy, carrots, chop suey greens, cilantro, corn salad, kale, kohlrabi, mizuna, oriental mustard greens, radicchio, radishes, scallions, spinach, Swiss chard, tarragon, winter lettuce

Plant: kale, leeks, strawberries

Harvest: American cress, apples, apricots, arugula, basil, beets, blackberries, blueberries, bokchoy, carrots, cherries, chicory, chili peppers, chives, chop suey greens, cilantro, corn, corn salad, cucumbers, currants, eggplants, endive, fennel, figs, Florence fennel, garlic, green beans, lettuce, microgreens, mint, mizuna, nectarines, spinach, onions, oregano, parsley, peaches, pears, peas, peppers, potatoes, radicchio, rosemary, runner beans, sage, shallots, tarragon, thyme, tomatoes, squashes, strawberries, zucchini

Shade

microgreens

save seeds!

My plans

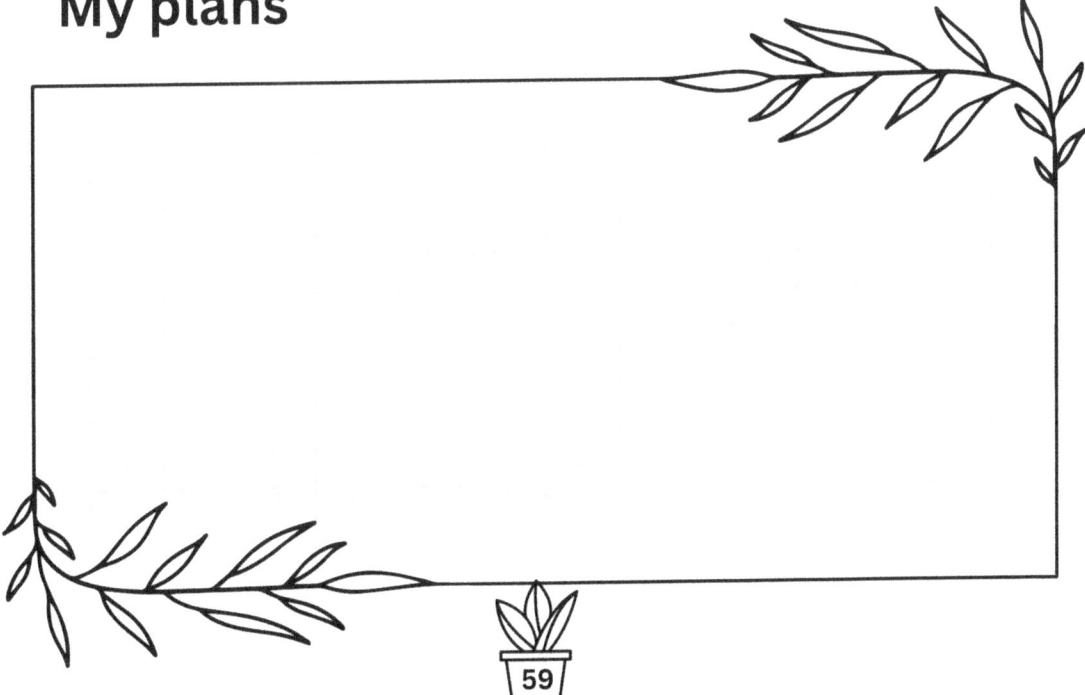

My Late Summer Tasks

Season:

Garden Beds/Row

- [ ]
- [ ]
- [ ]
- [ ]
- [ ]
- [ ]
- [ ]
- [ ]
- [ ]
- [ ]

Maintenance

- [ ]
- [ ]
- [ ]
- [ ]
- [ ]
- [ ]
- [ ]
- [ ]
- [ ]
- [ ]

Fertilizers

- [ ]
- [ ]
- [ ]
- [ ]
- [ ]
- [ ]
- [ ]
- [ ]
- [ ]
- [ ]

Planting/Harvesting

- [ ]
- [ ]
- [ ]
- [ ]
- [ ]
- [ ]
- [ ]
- [ ]
- [ ]
- [ ]

Seasonal Review: Summer

Plants harvested this season

Plants to try next season

What worked this season

What to do differently next season

Additional notes from this growing season

Seasonal Chore Planner

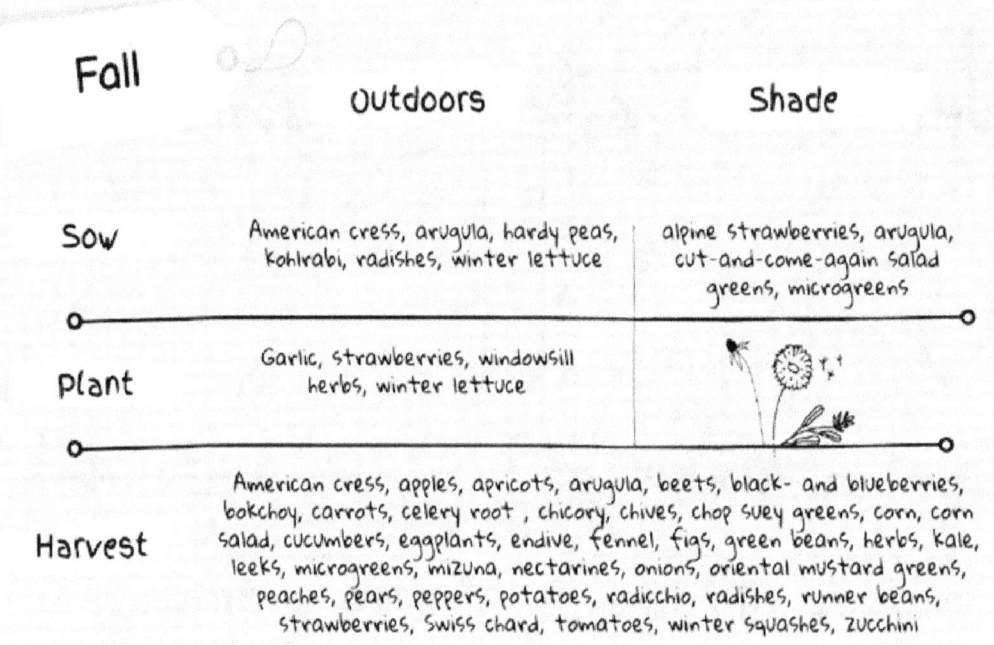

Fall	Outdoors	Shade
Sow	American cress, arugula, hardy peas, kohlrabi, radishes, winter lettuce	alpine strawberries, arugula, cut-and-come-again salad greens, microgreens
Plant	Garlic, strawberries, windowsill herbs, winter lettuce	
Harvest	American cress, apples, apricots, arugula, beets, black- and blueberries, bokchoy, carrots, celery root, chicory, chives, chop suey greens, corn, corn salad, cucumbers, eggplants, endive, fennel, figs, green beans, herbs, kale, leeks, microgreens, mizuna, nectarines, onions, oriental mustard greens, peaches, pears, peppers, potatoes, radicchio, radishes, runner beans, strawberries, Swiss chard, tomatoes, winter squashes, zucchini	

My plans

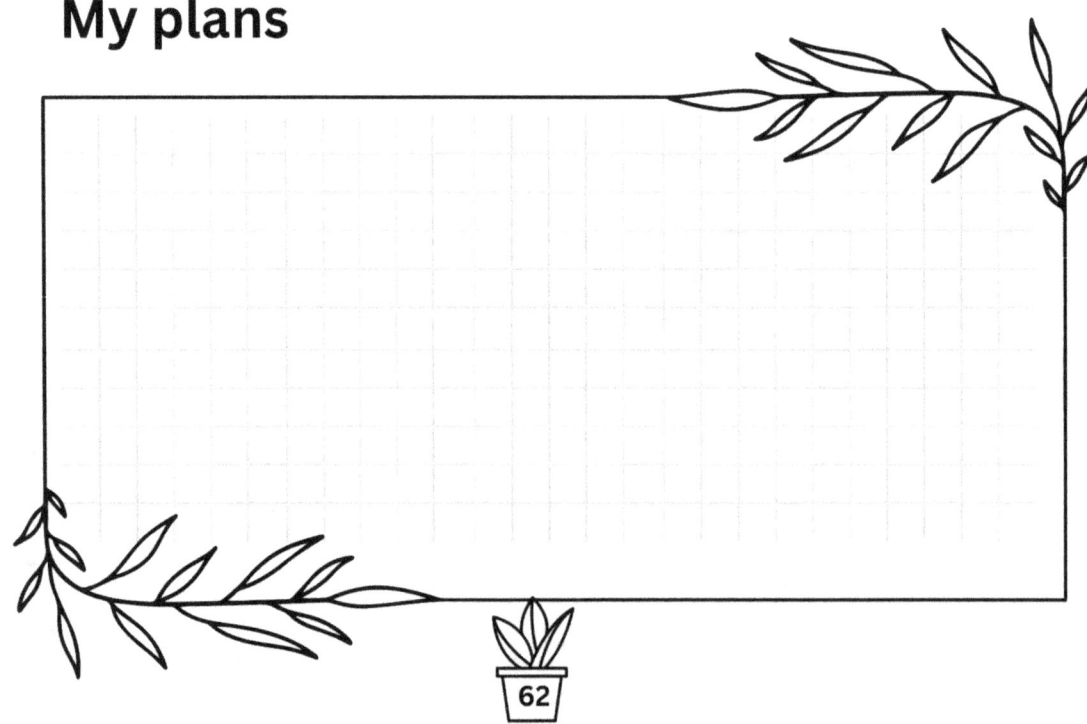

My Fall Tasks

Season:

Garden Beds/Row

- [ ]
- [ ]
- [ ]
- [ ]
- [ ]
- [ ]
- [ ]
- [ ]
- [ ]
- [ ]

Maintenance

- [ ]
- [ ]
- [ ]
- [ ]
- [ ]
- [ ]
- [ ]
- [ ]
- [ ]
- [ ]

Fertilizers

- [ ]
- [ ]
- [ ]
- [ ]
- [ ]
- [ ]
- [ ]
- [ ]
- [ ]
- [ ]

Planting/Harvesting

- [ ]
- [ ]
- [ ]
- [ ]
- [ ]
- [ ]
- [ ]
- [ ]
- [ ]
- [ ]

Seasonal review: Fall

Plants harvested this season

Plants to try next season

What worked this season

What to do differently next season

Additional notes from this growing season

Seasonal Chore Planner

Winter

	Outdoors	Shade
Sow	hardy peas	microgreens
Plant*	Fruit trees and bushes, garlic, rhubarb	
Harvest*	American cress, arugula, celery root, citrus fruits, corn salad, kale, leeks, microgreens, mizuna, oriental mustard greens, parsley, Swiss chard, thyme, windowsill herbs, winter lettuce, Witloof chicory	

* depends on your zone and microclimate!

My plans

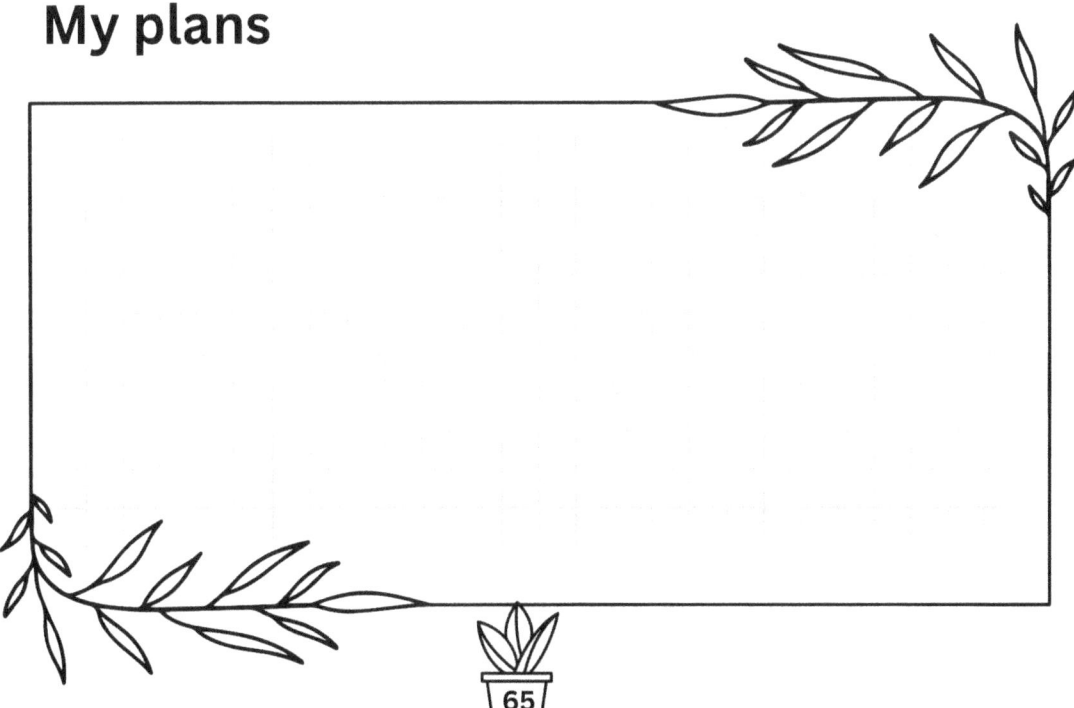

My Seasonal Tasks

Season:

Garden Beds/Row

- [ ]
- [ ]
- [ ]
- [ ]
- [ ]
- [ ]
- [ ]
- [ ]
- [ ]

Maintenance

- [ ]
- [ ]
- [ ]
- [ ]
- [ ]
- [ ]
- [ ]
- [ ]
- [ ]

Fertilizers

- [ ]
- [ ]
- [ ]
- [ ]
- [ ]
- [ ]
- [ ]
- [ ]
- [ ]

Planting/Harvesting

- [ ]
- [ ]
- [ ]
- [ ]
- [ ]
- [ ]
- [ ]
- [ ]
- [ ]

Seasonal review: Winter

Plants harvested this season

Plants to try next season

What worked this season

What to do differently next season

Additional notes from this growing season

Square-Foot Gardening Basics

Square-foot gardening is a simple and efficient way of growing plants. It's a variation of raised bed gardening. This method is ideal for beginner gardeners who want to grow more plants in a limited space.

You can start quickly by dividing a garden bed or a growing area into smaller one-foot squares. You can plant one, four, eight, nine, or more plants into each square, as you see below. It's also important to remember that different plants have different light, water, and nutrient needs.

For example, some plants need more sunlight than others, while some require regular watering to thrive. You can create a thriving garden in a small space by carefully selecting and grouping plants based on their needs.

Remember to check out the companion planting chart on page 74 to find the best buddies!

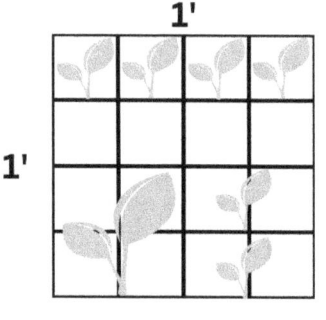

Square sizes and a simple conversion formula:

1 sq foot = 12" x 12" square
1 sq foot = appr. 30 x 30 cm

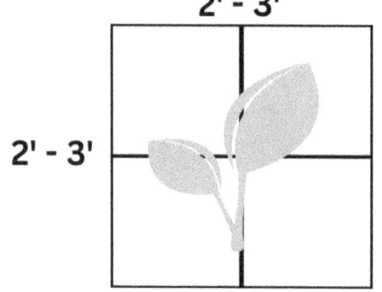

4 sq feet = 24" x 24" square
4 sq feet = appr. 60 x 60 cm

9 sq feet = 36" x 36" square
9 sq feet = appr. 90 x 90 cm

Square Foot Gardening Basics

**3" (7.5 cm) spacing
16 plants per sq foot**

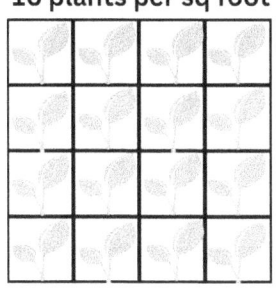

Radishes
Carrots
Beets

3" (7.5 cm) spacing - 8 plants per sq foot

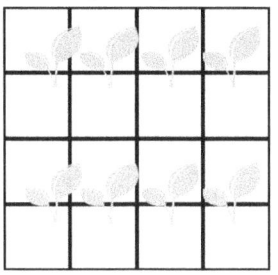

Pole beans
Green peas

**4" (10 cm) spacing
9 plants per sq foot**

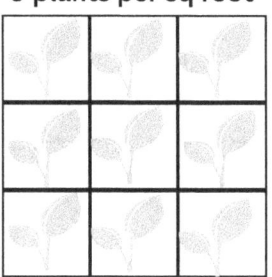

Spinach
Turnips
Scallions
Lettuce
Bush beans

6" (15 cm) spacing - 9 plants per sq foot

Parsley
Garlic
Leeks
Onions
Kohlrabi
Celeriac

**12" (30 cm) spacing
1 plant per sq foot**

Broccolii
Cabbage
Eggplant
Cucumber
Cauliflower
Corn
Peppers
Potatoes
Kale
Lettuce (head

**24" (60 cm) spacing
1 plant per 2 sq feet**

2'

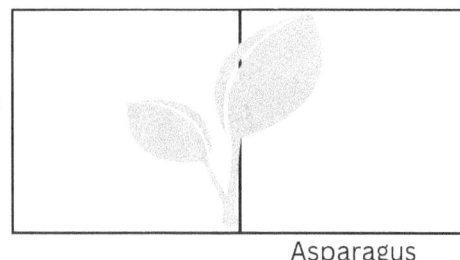

1'

Asparagus
Squash
(small, vining)

**24" (60 cm) spacing
1 plant per 4 sq feet**

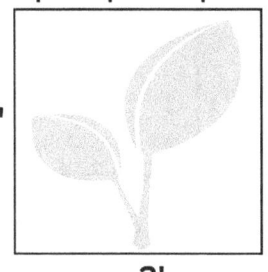

2'

2'

Melons
Tomatoes
Squash
(large, vining)

**36" (90 cm) spacing
1 plant per 9 sq feet**

3'

3'

Zucchini
Squash
(bush)

69

My Square Foot Garden

You can make the beds whatever length you want; just keep up the square structure.

My Square Foot garden

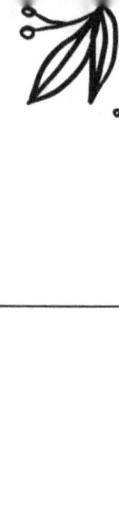

My Square Foot garden

My Square Foot garden

Companion Planting Quick Guide

Plant	Good companions	Bad companions
Asparagus	Basil, Marigold, Parsley, Dill, Tomato, Nasturtium	Garlic, Potato, Onions
Beans	Potato, Marigold, Cucumbers, Squash, Summer Savory, Corn	Tomato, Pepper, Chives, Garlic, Onions
Beets	Mint, Garlic, Onions, Leeks, Scallon, Broccoli, Cauliflower, Brussels sprouts, Radish, Kale, Cabbage	Pole beans
Broccoli	Dill, Mint, Rosemary	Strawberry, Mustard, Tomato, Oregano
Cabbage	Onions, Dill, Oregano, Sage, Mint, Chamomille, Nasturtium, Clover, Beets	Strawberry, Tomato, Peppers, Eggplant
Corn	Cucumber, Beans, Melons, Parsley, Squash, Marigold, Pumpkin	Tomato
Cucumber	Radish, Lettuce, Onions, Dill, Nasturtium, Corn, Beans	Potato, Sage
Eggplant	Catnip, Spinach, Peppers, Nasturtium, Marigold, Sunflower, Bush beans, Thyme, Tarragon, Tomato, Potato	Fennel
Lettuce	Radish, Dill, Cucumber, Carrot, Strawberry	Beans, Beets, Cabbage, Parsley
Peppers	Beans, Tomato, Onions, Geranium, Petunia	Fennel
Potato	Eggplant, Beans, Cabbage, Peas, Sage, Corn, Nasturtium, Catnip, Coriander	Cucumber, Tomato, Pumpkin, Spinach, Fennel, Onions, Squash, Fennel, Raspberries
Pumpkin	Melons, Corn, Dill, Radish, Beans, Oregano	Potato
Spinach	Cauliflower, Strawberry, Radish, Eggplant	Potato
Squash	Onion, Corn, Mint, Nasturtium, Dill, Peas, Beans, Radish	Potato
Tomato	Carrot, Parsley, Basil, Marigold, Garlic, Asparagus, Collards	Corn, Cabbage, Broccoli, Brussels sprouts, Potato
Turnip	Radish, Cauliflower, Beans, Lettuce, Spinach, Broccoli, Cabbage, Peas, Tomato, Brussels sprouts, Mint	Carrot, Parsley and other root crops
Zucchini	Nasturtium, Corn, Beans	Potato

Notes

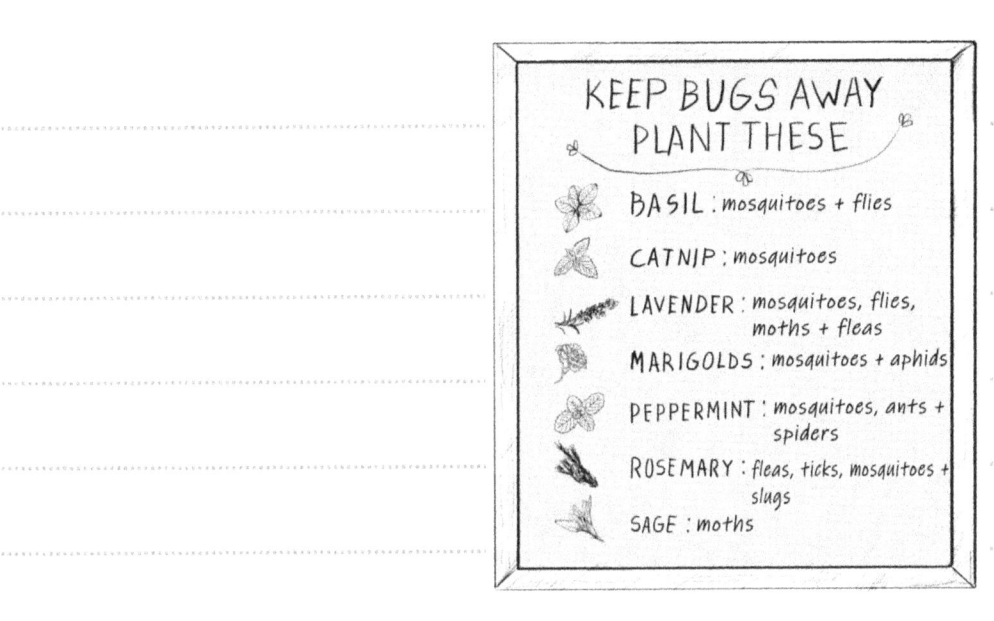

Notes

Crop Rotation Plan

Why is crop rotation a good idea?

Crop rotation is a technique that gardeners and farmers use to improve soil health, reduce pest and disease pressure, and increase crop yields.

By rotating the types of crops grown in a particular area over time, the soil can recover from the depletion of nutrients and build-up of pathogens that can occur when the same crops are grown in the same spot year after year.

Additionally, crop rotation can help break the life cycles of pests and diseases that may target specific crops, reducing the need for chemical interventions. Overall, this is a sustainable and effective way to maintain the health and productivity of a garden or farm.

Bed/Row/Square	Crop name	Season	Next crop to plant

Crop rotation plan

Keeping track of crop rotations will help you design your garden next year!

Bed/Row/Square	Crop name	Season	Next crop to plant

Crop rotation plan

Keeping track of crop rotations will help you design your garden next year!

Bed/Row/Square	Crop name	Season	Next crop to plant

Grow Bag Cheat Sheet

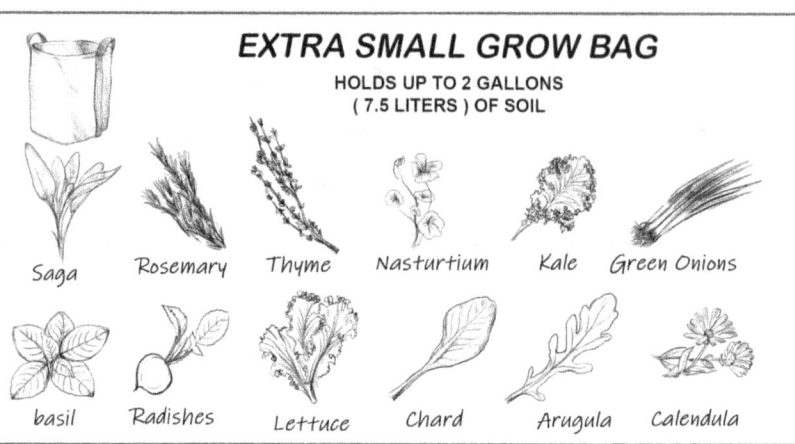

EXTRA SMALL GROW BAG
HOLDS UP TO 2 GALLONS
(7.5 LITERS) OF SOIL

Saga, Rosemary, Thyme, Nasturtium, Kale, Green Onions, basil, Radishes, Lettuce, Chard, Arugula, Calendula

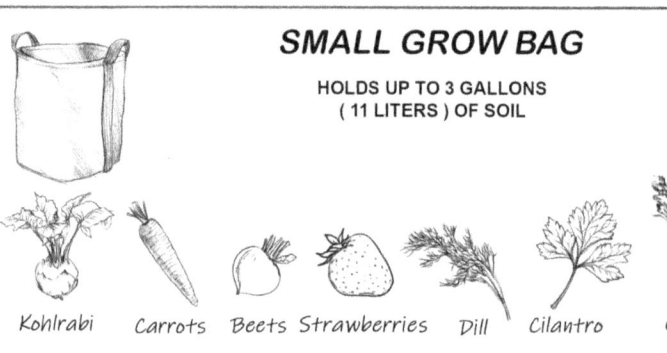

SMALL GROW BAG
HOLDS UP TO 3 GALLONS
(11 LITERS) OF SOIL

Kohlrabi, Carrots, Beets, Strawberries, Dill, Cilantro, Celery

MEDIUM GROW BAG
HOLDS UP TO 5 GALLONS
(19 LITERS) OF SOIL

Beans, Broccoli, Cabbage, lemongrass, Okra, Potatoes, Cucumbers, Eggplant, Peppers, Ginger, Turmeric

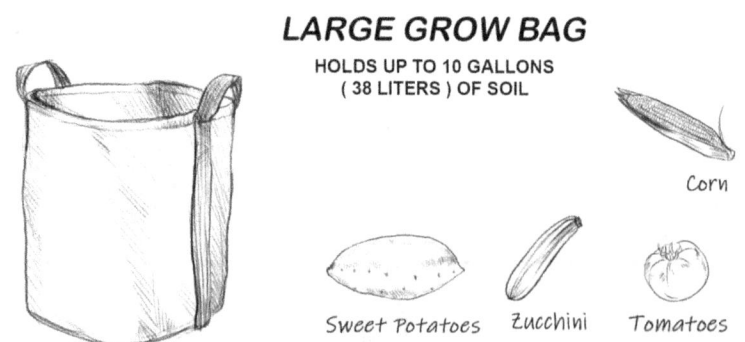

LARGE GROW BAG
HOLDS UP TO 10 GALLONS
(38 LITERS) OF SOIL

Corn, Sweet Potatoes, Zucchini, Tomatoes

Notes

Plant Profiles

PLANT NAME ....

| FLOWER ☐ VEGETABLE ☐ FRUIT ☐ HERB ☐ TREE ☐ SHRUB ☐ |
| SEEDLING ☐ BULB ☐ ANNUAL ☐ BIENNIAL ☐ PERENNIAL ☐ |

Plant source	
Purchase date	
Cost	

TIMETABLE

GERMINATION DATE	
PLANTING DATE	
TRANSPLANT DATE	
BLOOM DATE	
HARVEST DATE	
HARVEST TOTAL	
SEED SAVING DATE	
SEEDS DUE DATE	

PLANT NEEDS

LOCATION	
SUN	☀ ☀ ☀ ☀ ☀
WATER NEED	💧 💧 💧 💧 💧
HUMIDITY	
FERTILIZERS	
SOIL AMENDMENT	
RATE YOUR PLANT	🍃 🍃 🍃 🍃 🍃

NOTES

....
....
....
....
....
....
....

PESTS - WEEDS - DISEASES - SOLUTIONS

Plant Profiles

PLANT NAME ....

FLOWER ☐ VEGETABLE ☐ FRUIT ☐ HERB ☐ TREE ☐ SHRUB ☐ SEEDLING ☐ BULB ☐ ANNUAL ☐ BIENNIAL ☐ PERENNIAL ☐	
Plant source	
Purchase date	
Cost	

TIMETABLE	
GERMINATION DATE	
PLANTING DATE	
TRANSPLANT DATE	
BLOOM DATE	
HARVEST DATE	
HARVEST TOTAL	
SEED SAVING DATE	
SEEDS DUE DATE	

PLANT NEEDS	
LOCATION	
SUN	☀ ☀ ☀ ☀ ☀
WATER NEED	💧 💧 💧 💧 💧
HUMIDITY	
FERTILIZERS	
SOIL AMENDMENT	
RATE YOUR PLANT	🙂 🙂 🙂 🙂 🙂

NOTES

....
....
....
....
....
....
....

PESTS - WEEDS - DISEASES - SOLUTIONS

83

Plant Profiles

PLANT NAME ....

	FLOWER ☐	VEGETABLE ☐	FRUIT ☐	HERB ☐	TREE ☐	SHRUB ☐
	SEEDLING ☐	BULB ☐	ANNUAL ☐	BIENNIAL ☐	PERENNIAL ☐	

Plant source	
Purchase date	
Cost	

TIMETABLE

GERMINATION DATE	
PLANTING DATE	
TRANSPLANT DATE	
BLOOM DATE	
HARVEST DATE	
HARVEST TOTAL	
SEED SAVING DATE	
SEEDS DUE DATE	

PLANT NEEDS

LOCATION	
SUN	☼ ☼ ☼ ☼ ☼
WATER NEED	💧 💧 💧 💧 💧
HUMIDITY	
FERTILIZERS	
SOIL AMENDMENT	
RATE YOUR PLANT	🍃 🍃 🍃 🍃 🍃

NOTES

....
....
....
....
....
....
....

PESTS - WEEDS - DISEASES - SOLUTIONS

Plant Profiles

PLANT NAME ....

FLOWER ☐ VEGETABLE ☐ FRUIT ☐ HERB ☐ TREE ☐ SHRUB ☐ SEEDLING ☐ BULB ☐ ANNUAL ☐ BIENNIAL ☐ PERENNIAL ☐	
Plant source	
Purchase date	
Cost	

TIMETABLE

GERMINATION DATE	
PLANTING DATE	
TRANSPLANT DATE	
BLOOM DATE	
HARVEST DATE	
HARVEST TOTAL	
SEED SAVING DATE	
SEEDS DUE DATE	

PLANT NEEDS

LOCATION	
SUN	☀ ☀ ☀ ☀
WATER NEED	💧 💧 💧 💧 💧
HUMIDITY	
FERTILIZERS	
SOIL AMENDMENT	
RATE YOUR PLANT	

NOTES

....
....
....
....
....
....
....

PESTS - WEEDS - DISEASES - SOLUTIONS

Plant Profiles

PLANT NAME ....

FLOWER ☐ VEGETABLE ☐ FRUIT ☐ HERB ☐ TREE ☐ SHRUB ☐ SEEDLING ☐ BULB ☐ ANNUAL ☐ BIENNIAL ☐ PERENNIAL ☐	
Plant source	
Purchase date	
Cost	

TIMETABLE

GERMINATION DATE	
PLANTING DATE	
TRANSPLANT DATE	
BLOOM DATE	
HARVEST DATE	
HARVEST TOTAL	
SEED SAVING DATE	
SEEDS DUE DATE	

PLANT NEEDS

LOCATION	
SUN	☼ ☼ ☼ ☼ ☼
WATER NEED	💧 💧 💧 💧 💧
HUMIDITY	
FERTILIZERS	
SOIL AMENDMENT	
RATE YOUR PLANT	🍃 🍃 🍃 🍃 🍃

NOTES

....
....
....
....
....
....
....

PESTS – WEEDS – DISEASES – SOLUTIONS

Plant Profiles

PLANT NAME ....

FLOWER ☐ VEGETABLE ☐ FRUIT ☐ HERB ☐ TREE ☐ SHRUB ☐ SEEDLING ☐ BULB ☐ ANNUAL ☐ BIENNIAL ☐ PERENNIAL ☐	
Plant source	
Purchase date	
Cost	

TIMETABLE

GERMINATION DATE	
PLANTING DATE	
TRANSPLANT DATE	
BLOOM DATE	
HARVEST DATE	
HARVEST TOTAL	
SEED SAVING DATE	
SEEDS DUE DATE	

PLANT NEEDS

LOCATION	
SUN	☀ ☀ ☀ ☀ ☀
WATER NEED	💧 💧 💧 💧 💧
HUMIDITY	
FERTILIZERS	
SOIL AMENDMENT	
RATE YOUR PLANT	

NOTES

....
....
....
....
....
....
....

PESTS - WEEDS - DISEASES - SOLUTIONS

Plant Profiles

PLANT NAME ....

FLOWER ☐	VEGETABLE ☐	FRUIT ☐	HERB ☐	TREE ☐	SHRUB ☐
SEEDLING ☐	BULB ☐	ANNUAL ☐	BIENNIAL ☐	PERENNIAL ☐	

Plant source	
Purchase date	
Cost	

TIMETABLE

GERMINATION DATE	
PLANTING DATE	
TRANSPLANT DATE	
BLOOM DATE	
HARVEST DATE	
HARVEST TOTAL	
SEED SAVING DATE	
SEEDS DUE DATE	

PLANT NEEDS

LOCATION	
SUN	☀ ☀ ☀ ☀ ☀
WATER NEED	💧 💧 💧 💧 💧
HUMIDITY	
FERTILIZERS	
SOIL AMENDMENT	
RATE YOUR PLANT	🍃 🍃 🍃 🍃 🍃

NOTES

....
....
....
....
....
....
....

PESTS - WEEDS - DISEASES - SOLUTIONS

Plant Profiles

PLANT NAME ....

FLOWER ☐ VEGETABLE ☐ FRUIT ☐ HERB ☐ TREE ☐ SHRUB ☐ SEEDLING ☐ BULB ☐ ANNUAL ☐ BIENNIAL ☐ PERENNIAL ☐	

Plant source	
Purchase date	
Cost	

TIMETABLE	
GERMINATION DATE	
PLANTING DATE	
TRANSPLANT DATE	
BLOOM DATE	
HARVEST DATE	
HARVEST TOTAL	
SEED SAVING DATE	
SEEDS DUE DATE	

PLANT NEEDS	
LOCATION	
SUN	☀ ☀ ☀ ☀ ☀
WATER NEED	💧 💧 💧 💧 💧
HUMIDITY	
FERTILIZERS	
SOIL AMENDMENT	
RATE YOUR PLANT	☺ ☺ ☺ ☺ ☺

NOTES

....
....
....
....
....
....
....

PESTS - WEEDS - DISEASES - SOLUTIONS

Plant Profiles

PLANT NAME ....

FLOWER ☐ VEGETABLE ☐ FRUIT ☐ HERB ☐ TREE ☐ SHRUB ☐ SEEDLING ☐ BULB ☐ ANNUAL ☐ BIENNIAL ☐ PERENNIAL ☐	
Plant source	
Purchase date	
Cost	

TIMETABLE

GERMINATION DATE	
PLANTING DATE	
TRANSPLANT DATE	
BLOOM DATE	
HARVEST DATE	
HARVEST TOTAL	
SEED SAVING DATE	
SEEDS DUE DATE	

PLANT NEEDS

LOCATION	
SUN	☀ ☀ ☀ ☀ ☀
WATER NEED	💧 💧 💧 💧 💧
HUMIDITY	
FERTILIZERS	
SOIL AMENDMENT	
RATE YOUR PLANT	🍃 🍃 🍃 🍃 🍃

NOTES

....
....
....
....
....
....

PESTS - WEEDS - DISEASES - SOLUTIONS

Plant Profiles

PLANT NAME ....

FLOWER ☐ VEGETABLE ☐ FRUIT ☐ HERB ☐ TREE ☐ SHRUB ☐		
SEEDLING ☐ BULB ☐ ANNUAL ☐ BIENNIAL ☐ PERENNIAL ☐		

Plant source	
Purchase date	
Cost	

TIMETABLE

GERMINATION DATE	
PLANTING DATE	
TRANSPLANT DATE	
BLOOM DATE	
HARVEST DATE	
HARVEST TOTAL	
SEED SAVING DATE	
SEEDS DUE DATE	

PLANT NEEDS

LOCATION	
SUN	☀ ☀ ☀ ☀ ☀
WATER NEED	💧 💧 💧 💧 💧
HUMIDITY	
FERTILIZERS	
SOIL AMENDMENT	
RATE YOUR PLANT	

NOTES

....
....
....
....
....
....
....

PESTS - WEEDS - DISEASES - SOLUTIONS

Plant Profiles

PLANT NAME ....

FLOWER ☐ VEGETABLE ☐ FRUIT ☐ HERB ☐ TREE ☐ SHRUB ☐ SEEDLING ☐ BULB ☐ ANNUAL ☐ BIENNIAL ☐ PERENNIAL ☐	
Plant source	
Purchase date	
Cost	

TIMETABLE

GERMINATION DATE	
PLANTING DATE	
TRANSPLANT DATE	
BLOOM DATE	
HARVEST DATE	
HARVEST TOTAL	
SEED SAVING DATE	
SEEDS DUE DATE	

PLANT NEEDS

LOCATION	
SUN	☀ ☀ ☀ ☀ ☀
WATER NEED	💧 💧 💧 💧 💧
HUMIDITY	
FERTILIZERS	
SOIL AMENDMENT	
RATE YOUR PLANT	🍃 🍃 🍃 🍃 🍃

NOTES

....
....
....
....
....
....
....

PESTS - WEEDS - DISEASES - SOLUTIONS

Plant Profiles

PLANT NAME ....

FLOWER ☐ VEGETABLE ☐ FRUIT ☐ HERB ☐ TREE ☐ SHRUB ☐ SEEDLING ☐ BULB ☐ ANNUAL ☐ BIENNIAL ☐ PERENNIAL ☐	
Plant source	
Purchase date	
Cost	

TIMETABLE	
GERMINATION DATE	
PLANTING DATE	
TRANSPLANT DATE	
BLOOM DATE	
HARVEST DATE	
HARVEST TOTAL	
SEED SAVING DATE	
SEEDS DUE DATE	

PLANT NEEDS	
LOCATION	
SUN	☀ ☀ ☀ ☀ ☀
WATER NEED	💧 💧 💧 💧 💧
HUMIDITY	
FERTILIZERS	
SOIL AMENDMENT	
RATE YOUR PLANT	☺ ☺ ☺ ☺ ☺

NOTES

....
....
....
....
....
....

PESTS - WEEDS - DISEASES - SOLUTIONS

Plant Profiles

PLANT NAME ....

FLOWER ☐ VEGETABLE ☐ FRUIT ☐ HERB ☐ TREE ☐ SHRUB ☐ SEEDLING ☐ BULB ☐ ANNUAL ☐ BIENNIAL ☐ PERENNIAL ☐	
Plant source	
Purchase date	
Cost	

TIMETABLE

GERMINATION DATE	
PLANTING DATE	
TRANSPLANT DATE	
BLOOM DATE	
HARVEST DATE	
HARVEST TOTAL	
SEED SAVING DATE	
SEEDS DUE DATE	

PLANT NEEDS

LOCATION	
SUN	☀ ☀ ☀ ☀ ☀
WATER NEED	💧 💧 💧 💧 💧
HUMIDITY	
FERTILIZERS	
SOIL AMENDMENT	
RATE YOUR PLANT	🍃 🍃 🍃 🍃 🍃

NOTES

....
....
....
....
....
....
....

PESTS – WEEDS – DISEASES – SOLUTIONS

Plant Profiles

PLANT NAME ....

FLOWER ☐ VEGETABLE ☐ FRUIT ☐ HERB ☐ TREE ☐ SHRUB ☐ SEEDLING ☐ BULB ☐ ANNUAL ☐ BIENNIAL ☐ PERENNIAL ☐	
Plant source	
Purchase date	
Cost	

TIMETABLE

GERMINATION DATE	
PLANTING DATE	
TRANSPLANT DATE	
BLOOM DATE	
HARVEST DATE	
HARVEST TOTAL	
SEED SAVING DATE	
SEEDS DUE DATE	

PLANT NEEDS

LOCATION	
SUN	☀ ☀ ☀ ☀ ☀
WATER NEED	💧 💧 💧 💧 💧
HUMIDITY	
FERTILIZERS	
SOIL AMENDMENT	
RATE YOUR PLANT	🍃 🍃 🍃 🍃 🍃

NOTES

....
....
....
....
....
....
....

PESTS - WEEDS - DISEASES - SOLUTIONS

Plant Profiles

PLANT NAME ....

FLOWER ☐ VEGETABLE ☐ FRUIT ☐ HERB ☐ TREE ☐ SHRUB ☐ SEEDLING ☐ BULB ☐ ANNUAL ☐ BIENNIAL ☐ PERENNIAL ☐	
Plant source	
Purchase date	
Cost	

TIMETABLE

GERMINATION DATE	
PLANTING DATE	
TRANSPLANT DATE	
BLOOM DATE	
HARVEST DATE	
HARVEST TOTAL	
SEED SAVING DATE	
SEEDS DUE DATE	

PLANT NEEDS

LOCATION	
SUN	☀ ☀ ☀ ☀ ☀
WATER NEED	💧 💧 💧 💧 💧
HUMIDITY	
FERTILIZERS	
SOIL AMENDMENT	
RATE YOUR PLANT	🍃 🍃 🍃 🍃 🍃

NOTES

....
....
....
....
....
....
....

PESTS - WEEDS - DISEASES - SOLUTIONS

Plant Profiles

PLANT NAME ....

FLOWER ☐ VEGETABLE ☐ FRUIT ☐ HERB ☐ TREE ☐ SHRUB ☐ SEEDLING ☐ BULB ☐ ANNUAL ☐ BIENNIAL ☐ PERENNIAL ☐	
Plant source	
Purchase date	
Cost	

TIMETABLE

GERMINATION DATE	
PLANTING DATE	
TRANSPLANT DATE	
BLOOM DATE	
HARVEST DATE	
HARVEST TOTAL	
SEED SAVING DATE	
SEEDS DUE DATE	

PLANT NEEDS

LOCATION	
SUN	☀ ☀ ☀ ☀ ☀
WATER NEED	💧 💧 💧 💧 💧
HUMIDITY	
FERTILIZERS	
SOIL AMENDMENT	
RATE YOUR PLANT	🙂 🙂 🙂 🙂 🙂

NOTES

....
....
....
....
....
....

PESTS - WEEDS - DISEASES - SOLUTIONS

Plant Profiles

PLANT NAME ....

FLOWER ☐ VEGETABLE ☐ FRUIT ☐ HERB ☐ TREE ☐ SHRUB ☐ SEEDLING ☐ BULB ☐ ANNUAL ☐ BIENNIAL ☐ PERENNIAL ☐	
Plant source	
Purchase date	
Cost	

TIMETABLE	
GERMINATION DATE	
PLANTING DATE	
TRANSPLANT DATE	
BLOOM DATE	
HARVEST DATE	
HARVEST TOTAL	
SEED SAVING DATE	
SEEDS DUE DATE	

PLANT NEEDS	
LOCATION	
SUN	☀ ☀ ☀ ☀ ☀
WATER NEED	💧 💧 💧 💧 💧
HUMIDITY	
FERTILIZERS	
SOIL AMENDMENT	
RATE YOUR PLANT	🍃 🍃 🍃 🍃 🍃

NOTES

....
....
....
....
....
....
....

PESTS - WEEDS - DISEASES - SOLUTIONS

Plant Profiles

PLANT NAME ....

FLOWER ☐	VEGETABLE ☐	FRUIT ☐	HERB ☐	TREE ☐	SHRUB ☐	
SEEDLING ☐	BULB ☐	ANNUAL ☐	BIENNIAL ☐	PERENNIAL ☐		

Plant source	
Purchase date	
Cost	

TIMETABLE

GERMINATION DATE	
PLANTING DATE	
TRANSPLANT DATE	
BLOOM DATE	
HARVEST DATE	
HARVEST TOTAL	
SEED SAVING DATE	
SEEDS DUE DATE	

PLANT NEEDS

LOCATION	
SUN	☀ ☀ ☀ ☀ ☀
WATER NEED	💧 💧 💧 💧 💧
HUMIDITY	
FERTILIZERS	
SOIL AMENDMENT	
RATE YOUR PLANT	☺ ☺ ☺ ☺ ☺

NOTES

....
....
....
....
....
....
....

PESTS - WEEDS - DISEASES - SOLUTIONS

Plant Profiles

PLANT NAME ....

| FLOWER ☐ VEGETABLE ☐ FRUIT ☐ HERB ☐ TREE ☐ SHRUB ☐ |
| SEEDLING ☐ BULB ☐ ANNUAL ☐ BIENNIAL ☐ PERENNIAL ☐ |

Plant source	
Purchase date	
Cost	

TIMETABLE

GERMINATION DATE	
PLANTING DATE	
TRANSPLANT DATE	
BLOOM DATE	
HARVEST DATE	
HARVEST TOTAL	
SEED SAVING DATE	
SEEDS DUE DATE	

PLANT NEEDS

LOCATION	
SUN	☀ ☀ ☀ ☀ ☀
WATER NEED	💧 💧 💧 💧 💧
HUMIDITY	
FERTILIZERS	
SOIL AMENDMENT	
RATE YOUR PLANT	🍃 🍃 🍃 🍃 🍃

NOTES

....
....
....
....
....
....

PESTS - WEEDS - DISEASES - SOLUTIONS

Plant Profiles

PLANT NAME ....

FLOWER ☐ VEGETABLE ☐ FRUIT ☐ HERB ☐ TREE ☐ SHRUB ☐ SEEDLING ☐ BULB ☐ ANNUAL ☐ BIENNIAL ☐ PERENNIAL ☐	
Plant source	
Purchase date	
Cost	

TIMETABLE

GERMINATION DATE	
PLANTING DATE	
TRANSPLANT DATE	
BLOOM DATE	
HARVEST DATE	
HARVEST TOTAL	
SEED SAVING DATE	
SEEDS DUE DATE	

PLANT NEEDS

LOCATION	
SUN	☀ ☀ ☀ ☀ ☀
WATER NEED	💧 💧 💧 💧 💧
HUMIDITY	
FERTILIZERS	
SOIL AMENDMENT	
RATE YOUR PLANT	🙁 😕 😐 🙂 😊

NOTES

....
....
....
....
....
....
....

PESTS – WEEDS – DISEASES – SOLUTIONS

Plant Profiles

PLANT NAME ....

FLOWER ☐ VEGETABLE ☐ FRUIT ☐ HERB ☐ TREE ☐ SHRUB ☐ SEEDLING ☐ BULB ☐ ANNUAL ☐ BIENNIAL ☐ PERENNIAL ☐	
Plant source	
Purchase date	
Cost	

TIMETABLE	
GERMINATION DATE	
PLANTING DATE	
TRANSPLANT DATE	
BLOOM DATE	
HARVEST DATE	
HARVEST TOTAL	
SEED SAVING DATE	
SEEDS DUE DATE	

PLANT NEEDS	
LOCATION	
SUN	☼ ☼ ☼ ☼ ☼
WATER NEED	💧 💧 💧 💧 💧
HUMIDITY	
FERTILIZERS	
SOIL AMENDMENT	
RATE YOUR PLANT	🍃 🍃 🍃 🍃 🍃

NOTES

....
....
....
....
....
....
....

PESTS - WEEDS - DISEASES - SOLUTIONS

Composting Basics

Composting is the process of turning organic waste into nutrient-rich compost, which can be used to improve soil fertility and support healthy plant growth.

To start composting, **collect a mix of "green" materials and "brown" materials.** Layer these materials in a compost bin or pile, ensuring a good mix of carbon-rich browns and nitrogen-rich greens. It's important to maintain a moist (but not soggy) compost pile, regularly turning or aerating it to provide oxygen for the decomposition process.

As the materials break down, beneficial microorganisms and earthworms will naturally decompose the organic matter, turning it into nutrient-rich compost.

Browns & Greens
Sources for Compost

Brown Materials	Green Materials
Dried Grass	Grass Clippings
Shredded Paper	Kelp or Seaweed
100% Cotton Fabrics (small pieces)	Green Shrub Prunings
Cardboard Egg Cartons	Houseplants
Wrapping Paper	Weeds (without seed heads)
Paper Towels	Old Flower Bouquets
Straw	Human/ Animal Hair
Chipped Wood	Aquarium Water (freshwater only)
Newspaper	Tea Bags
Toilet Paper Rolls	Alfalfa Meal/Hay
Wood Ash(not coal)	Coffee Grounds/Filter
Dry, Shredded Leaves	Animal Manure (herbivores only)
Sawdust	Vegetable Trimmings
Aged Hay	Algae
Oat Hay	Green Leaves
Cardboard	

Notes

Rainfall Recording Sheet and Watering Tracker

Track the amount of rainfall by noting the measurements from your rain gauge or referring to official weather reports for your area. Document your watering activities as well.

Week	Monday	Tuesday	Wednesday	Thursday	Friday	Saturday	Sunday	Total for the week

Rainfall Recording Sheet and Watering Tracker

Track the amount of rainfall by noting the measurements from your rain gauge or referring to official weather reports for your area. Document your watering activities as well.

Week	Monday	Tuesday	Wednesday	Thursday	Friday	Saturday	Sunday	Total for the week

Rainfall Recording Sheet and Watering Tracker

Track the amount of rainfall by noting the measurements from your rain gauge or referring to official weather reports for your area. Document your watering activities as well.

Week	Monday	Tuesday	Wednesday	Thursday	Friday	Saturday	Sunday	Total for the week

Water Saving Ideas for the Future

Pest and Disease Tracker

Whenever you notice signs of pests or diseases in your garden, make a note of the date and the specific symptoms or damage observed. Be detailed in your descriptions, noting the affected plant species, the specific parts of the plant impacted, and any distinctive characteristics of the pest or disease.

Note any treatments, interventions, or organic remedies you apply, along with the date of each action. Monitor the progress and effectiveness of your treatments or interventions.

Make additional notes over time, recording any changes in the severity of the problem or improvements in the plant's health.

Pest / Disease	Plants affected	Problem	Treatment	Results

Pest and Disease Tracker

Pest / Disease	Plants affected	Problem	Treatment	Results

Pest and Disease Tracker

Pest / Disease	Plants affected	Problem	Treatment	Results

Pollinator Fan Page

When you see pollinators such as bees, butterflies or hummingbirds, note the date, the type of pollinator, and any specific observations about their behavior or preferences.

Keep track of the steps you take to invite and support pollinators in your garden. These might include planting pollinator-friendly flowers, providing water sources, or creating habitat features such as nesting sites or insect hotels.

Use the pollinator fan page to learn from their experiences. Identify which plants, features, or practices are most successful in attracting and supporting pollinators. Use this knowledge to further enhance your garden as a pollinator-friendly place.

Name: *Honeybees*
Date: *June + July*
Where: *Grandma's flower bed*
Notes: *they love lavenders!*

Name:
Date:
Where:
Notes:

Actions & results:
- We need more pollinator-friendly flowers next year
- Remember to provide fresh water for the birds & pollinators

Pollinator Fan Page

Name: .... Date: ....
Where: .... Notes: ....
....
....
....

Name: .... Date: ....
Where: .... Notes: ....
....
....
....

Name: .... Date: ....
Where: .... Notes: ....
....
....
....

Name: .... Date: ....
Where: .... Notes: ....
....
....
....

Pollinator Fan Page

Name: .... Date: ....
Where: .... Notes: ....
....
....
....

Name: .... Date: ....
Where: .... Notes: ....
....
....
....

Name: .... Date: ....
Where: .... Notes: ....
....
....
....

Actions & results:

Pollinator Fan Page

Name: .... Date: ....
Where: .... Notes: ....
....
....
....

Name: .... Date: ....
Where: .... Notes: ....
....
....
....

Name: .... Date: ....
Where: .... Notes: ....
....
....
....

Name: .... Date: ....
Where: .... Notes: ....
....
....
....

Pollinator Fan Page

Name: .... Date: ....
Where: .... Notes: ....
....
....
....

Name: .... Date: ....
Where: .... Notes: ....
....
....
....

Name: .... Date: ....
Where: .... Notes: ....
....
....
....

Actions & results:

Pollinator Fan Page

Name: .... Date: ....
Where: .... Notes: ....
....
....
....

Name: .... Date: ....
Where: .... Notes: ....
....
....
....

Name: .... Date: ....
Where: .... Notes: ....
....
....
....

Name: .... Date: ....
Where: .... Notes: ....
....
....
....

Pollinator Fan Page

Name: .... Date: ....
Where: .... Notes: ....
....
....
....

Name: .... Date: ....
Where: .... Notes: ....
....
....
....

Name: .... Date: ....
Where: .... Notes: ....
....
....
....

Actions & results:

Need more pages to track your garden's progress?

I've got good news for you!

Visit my website,
https://sophiemckay.com/free-resources/
to access and download free, printable pages.

These extra pages follow the same format as the book, ensuring **you can continue documenting your gardening journey with ease and familiarity**.

Whether you need more space for your planting timelines, pest control notes, or your latest garden layout ideas, these additional pages are ready to help you. **Expand your journal as your garden grows** because your green thumb adventure deserves unlimited space.

Happy gardening!

Sophie

Notes

Notes

Notes

Notes

Notes

Notes

Notes

Notes

Notes

Notes

Dot Grid Planner

Dot Grid Planner

Dot Grid Planner

Dot Grid Planner

Dot Grid Planner

Dot Grid Planner

Thanks for Reading; please leave a review!

I would be incredibly happy if you could rate my book or leave a review on Amazon.

Just scan this QR code with your phone, or visit the http://journal.sophiemckay.com link to land directly on the book's Amazon review page.

Your review not only helps me create better books but also helps more fellow gardeners experience success in the garden and put healthy food on their family's table.

Thank you!

Sophie

Ready for some more inspiration?

Check out Sophie's books to keep your garden thriving all year round. Create your own sustainable permaculture garden, or dive deep into container gardening with proven DIY methods for composting, companion planting, seed saving, water management and pest control!
Learn how to grow your own food in harmony with nature. Success is guaranteed!

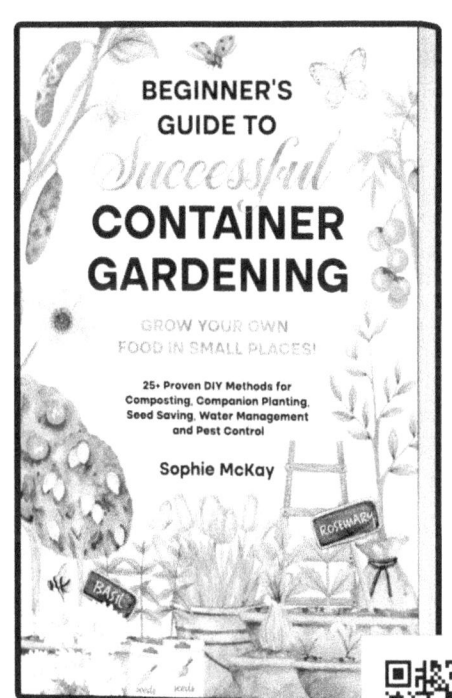 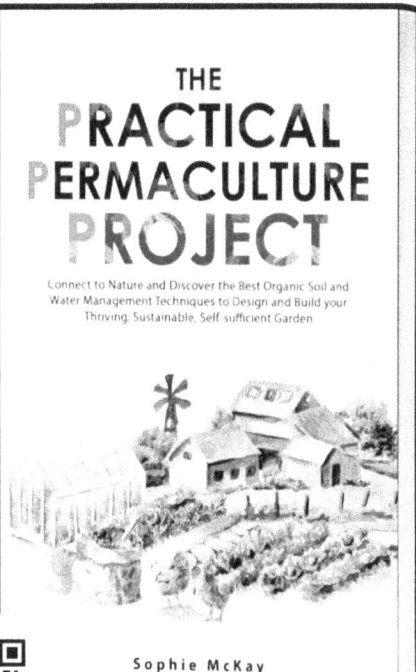

Just scan this QR code with your phone, or
visit the https://Series.SophieMckay.com link
to land directly on the book's Amazon page.

www.ingramcontent.com/pod-product-compliance
Lightning Source LLC
Chambersburg PA
CBHW081619100526
44590CB00021B/3514